A GRIP ON THIN AIR

Jane Griffiths

✸

A GRIP ON
THIN AIR

BLOODAXE BOOKS

Copyright © Jane Griffiths 2000

ISBN: 1 85224 539 5

First published 2000 by
Bloodaxe Books Ltd,
Highgreen,
Tarset,
Northumberland NE48 1RP.

Bloodaxe Books Ltd acknowledges
the financial assistance of Northern Arts.

Cover printing by J. Thomson Colour Printers Ltd, Glasgow.

Printed in Great Britain by
Cromwell Press Ltd, Trowbridge, Wiltshire.

But of that supposicyon that callyd is arte,
Confuse distributyve, as Parrot hath devysed,
Let every man after his merit take his parte.

JOHN SKELTON
Speke Parrot

Acknowledgements

Acknowledgements are due to the editors of the following publications in which some of these poems first appeared: *Arvon International Poetry Competition 1995 Anthology of Winning Poems* (Arvon Foundation, 1996), *Birdsuit, Magdalen Poets: An Anthology* (Magdalen, 2000), *New Blood* (Bloodaxe Books, 1999), *Oxford Poetry, The Rialto, The Ring of Words: Poems from the Daily Telegraph / Arvon International Poetry Competition 1998* (Sutton, 1998).

I would also like to thank the Society of Authors and their judges for an Eric Gregory Award in 1996, and Eastern Arts for a generous grant in 1992.

Contents

9   Migration
10   Arrival
11   The Skater
12   Norfolk
14   Emigrants
15   Story
16   Elemental
18   Island
20   A Haunted House
22   Beginning Her Journey
23   Flight-path
24   Metamorphosis
25   Women and Secrets
26   Love
27   Rumour
28   Perfect Pitch
30   Landscape
31   Likeness
32   Naming
33   Equilibrium
34   Polyptych: Annunciation
38   Equivocation
39   Bilingual
40   Because words are not things
41   Lost and Found
42   The Master-Builder
44   House
46   Travelling Light
47   Skelton and the Birds
48   Skelton at Diss
50   First Light
51   Hawk Point
52   From Barbara Hepworth's Garden
54   Shelf-Life/Life-writing
55   Speech
56   The Art of Memory
58   Abstract
60   Parallel Motion
61   A poem against the kind of occasional verse
62   Errata
64   The Biographies of Poets

Migration

First, there was the waking,
each day, to a lightness
they couldn't place. The air
stretched tight as a sheet;
the sun on their whitewashed

walls was flexible, or at any rate
warm and rounded to the touch.
It clung about them; they moved
shadowless, footsteps dropping like
stones to the light-resounding bay.

Daily their home gathered weed,
names, string. Sea-changed,
their eyes lost transparency;
they saw the house as it was:
a wholly new thing.

When the dreams came:
tarred and feathered bundles
of prehistory, their webbed feet
clay. They came overnight,
silently, as homing birds

to their owners, whose waking
each day was to a clogged grey
dawn, whose night-time shadows
had wings, scything steeply
above their narrow beds.

Arrival

Still travelling, he dreams up his arrival –
lime-green and mottled. Grey. There will be
boats, increasingly; first, an interruption
of the sea's languid splay, the engine
hesitantly changing its beat. There's no quay
in sight yet, but in the waves' slap-and-lull

a distant hint of land: a quiet, elemental
preparation for change. Meantime, shapes loom
suddenly; as suddenly vanish, unidentified:
tawny for buoys, rust for a dredger? Few guide-
lines here for the homing ear and eye. A gloom
descends on the sundeck. This is an interval;

the slow outreach of the bay, the predictable
greying cliffs and greyish rain. Harold's tomb
lies to the north, with above it a rise of tide-
marked fields. This is watercolour country, wide
reaches of drab rippled by offshore sound: boom
of light-ships, a siren gull. Houses are vertical:

white pinions to the land's falling off – impersonal.
If a door opens, and someone calls soundlessly
across the street, the ship's beneath her observation.
Its passengers are daily and bear no relation
to her, to whom the three dimensions of the estuary
are home, and arrivals a fourth, unremarkable.

The Skater

Quick against the dead
of landscape, a fluster
of movement with at its edges
hesitancy.

There's a fresh element
this winter: the water's
new solidity, which draws
an expectant cluster

of spectators, and one
in black, who pulls away
without effort, his track
long and powdery

parallels, cross-hatching.
And quick – such surety
in motion it's a vanishing
trick of the light,

as against the sun
between shoulder-high banks
his figure dwindles
across a country that's dark

and barely charted but
by the skates' straight lines
of passage. A territory
where fish show amber in ice,

their eyes unblinking under
the imprint of skates and sky,
roundly containing them:
curved and in miniature.

Norfolk

Drive-through country, between
the last inland stop and a promise
of the sea. The sky brims
with its approaching victory;

fields are its undertow,
converged on the middle distance where
poplars flaunt the river's
absence or an oak avenue

too abruptly ends. Young
corn springs brash as pins in its furrows
and slowly an over-
lifesized scarecrow swings its shadow

over a gathering
of pigeons and roll-gait gulls. Its dull
creaking plumbs the sky, while
the two-tone whistle of passing

geese beats out the bounds of
the horizon and at the field's edge
the first train rackets by.
Mornings, the country is testing

its limits, but at dusk
the corn's a deep grey weight of shadow,
fields lying low beneath
dark and sentinel trees, waiting

for the night to draw in
like a sea-mist, undoing distance
and making of houses,
lighthouses over ebbing fields.

Where, lying awake, you
might almost hear the red-smocked scarecrow
shifting (each morning he's
slightly further off) and an owl

whose hunting call drifts long
and horizontally while houses
lie like echoes under
the vocal strata of the sky.

Emigrants

Will know where they are by the absence
of trees, of people – the absence
even of anything to do. All
luggage is in transit; nothing at all
to do but watch from the empty house

through the empty window. The sky
is underlit, and under the sky
a lake; pewter, reflecting. A road.
Yellow buses turn at the end of the road,
if it is an end. Reeds block the view.

This bus is wheel-deep in them; it swims
along the lake's edge and a swan swims
towards it. They pass. And here, at last,
are two people, waiting for the last
bus out, or just standing, as people must

stand here often, leaning on the wind,
deep in reeds, and speechless in the wind
as if *lake* and *sky* were foreign words
to them as well: standing without words
but without need of them, being at home.

Story

They came on a breezy day
and a bright one, the house
rubicund in its circle of corn.
They came with brushes
and hampers and a cat
at their heels. The windows
were star-struck; the cat
shot straight through, out
into the passing cumulus.

The walls were papered and they
painted them. The floors were
lino: they engaged battle.
In the garden the corn whistled
sharp as steel. There was a pump;
there was a honeycomb of bricks
round the well. There were coppers,
histories and beehives. They dug
a pond. The cat went missing.

They beat the bounds and the geese
flew over; the walls were crumbling
and they mortared them. (Between
narrow bricks, lime shrilled in
emphatic punctuation.) At night,
the chimney stuck out like a sore thumb;
the house grew crooked as lightning.
They dug themselves in, they threw
out the ballast. They carried on.

Elemental

Lowlands. The air is liquid with rain
that doesn't fall; the sun hangs in suspension.
Light is seeping away down the track
that runs like a tightrope
from Krimpen to Ouderkerk, glistening
black between black, glistening, untranslatable
sloten (slots, cuts, or drainage ditches?

– they are not canals). Two cyclists pass.
The track hisses like a live wire; tyremarks crass
silver on black. The air's saturate.
With speed, colour bleeds from
their backs: swimming, scarlet, a comet's
tail. There are tidemarks strung out across the sky;
the water is rising. A heron hoists

itself, weightily, into thin air;
its counterpart goes down, an underwater
cloud blocking the underwater sun.
Land's down to a float-line
between two elements, is rarely
firm or *dry* (on a flood-tide, pavements ripple
in formation) except when, winters,
frost seals it in; skaters
take to the roads like water, cutting
across roof-tops, circling the upstairs windows
of houses grounded solidly on

their own reflections between paint-brush
poplars and crescented fish, over a pale
sun which marks time against the under-
side of the ice. The air's
so crackled with frost it seems it too
would bear and even the town's red-brick frontage
looks firm, like a destination.

But the thaw will begin at night on
the river high above town; it will come in
like an act of translation with wind
from the west in tidal
waves, sounding off roofs and ridge-tiles like
ships' wooden hulls, like ice floes overhead or
the full, reflected moon rebounding.

Island

Waking, the sounds come first, amorphous
and discordant as
an orchestra tuning.
The mist is banked against the house like snow;
the house is feathered and embedded in it:
it is drifting

(slowly) back to sleep, while somewhere down
below the cloud, day
is finding its voice, piece
by crystalline piece: the five goslings stir,
the gander goes off like a soda siphon
at imagined

alarms and diversions, Vienna
the mare is breezing
in her stall, and beyond
the garden wall, a Range Rover goes by
quivering antennae, with its radio
tuning in to

England, where *it is eight o'clock*
on Thursday, the twelfth
of June. From the window
cropped-off roofs and conifers appear where
France or Guernsey might be on a brighter day.
(It's not clear what

the point of the view is.) Although down
in the valleys this
could almost be mainland,
out on the coast-road improvisation
hangs on in a breeze-block trellis that trebles
as balcony

wine-rack, boot and geranium stand;
in German bunkers
turned fish-farm and in all
the *cotils* where potato leaves flurry
in arrested waterfalls over the roofs
and bantams pass

behind the chimneys: even the land's
doubled up. Out at
the Fisherman's Chapel
in St Brelade, wall-paintings show coffins
open for the Resurrection (more like boats
or hip-baths than

terra firma coffins) putting out
in a whitewash sea.
Of Christ, just head and limbs
remain: like rocks, like the islanded limbs
of a sleeper. Hands clasped, the buoyant, painted
dead break out of

the stone as if for air, making their
representations
fervently, forever,
while in the main church a placard
commands visitors' prayers, and across the bay
the twice-daily

ferry bluffs its way out through the fog
which may be general
or may be a local
challenge to all comers, like the sign at
the Methodist Chapel that claims (stony-faced)
Truth Is Inside.

A Haunted House

There are clues everywhere.
A caravan is parked
in the old parlour.
They are growing thyme
and tarragon against the wall.

Someone is out, calling
the animals. Indoors,
alcoves lead to nothing
in particular. A blocked
window above the stairs,

traces of half-timbering
over the hall. In the green
room, remains of Regency
wallpaper: fleur-de-lis
on eau-de-nil. A backdrop.

The hunt is off the scent
in the long gallery; dogs
raise their noses from a tide
of whitewashed reeds.
Nothing is only itself:

the house is a sampler.
In an early engraving
a man in a morning-coat
retreats swiftly into the hall.
The chimney is crooked already;

the curved white mermaids
over the door watch swimmingly
over the fields, which are their fields,
over the farm. The sun is setting
through the orchard; someone

is out, calling the animals.
Like drought-photography,
sun-down reveals the line
of the moat, the foundations
of a barn. And the animals,

taking the place in their stride:
an eyeful of peacocks trampling
the tarragon; sheep flowing
through the stony moat,
squaring up to the vanished

yard. The dead cats, Quince,
Olly and Ragtime are dancing
like light over bricks left out
to dry for the first building
of the hall. Doves pass over

in a loose-leaved fan;
rooks gather round the oaks
in the moat. The sky is dark
with cries; they are all out
calling the animals, but

the sun forges walls to red
umber, to burnt sienna, and tilts
at windows as if, given purchase,
it would course through the house
as through a shell, emblazoning

rafters and licking life into
the painted dogs in the gallery
until they too give tongue,
raising the roof and calling,
calling the animals home.

Beginning Her Journey

(after a wood-engraving by Anne Hayward)

The portents are mixed. She has achieved a corner seat
facing the engine, but by the sheer weight of it, the sun
must be setting. This means she is travelling east.

It is clearly winter. Outside the window, trees articulate
the air. The glass is thin: the long grasses seem almost
in the carriage, and branches teasle the gap between

the door and the door's reduced reflection on the far
side of the track. The cropped field is stubbly and plush as
the upholstery. She has a prickling in the back of the knees

and a basket, and a wary look. Her hair is cut precisely
as the grass, each fine white mark a defining act,
irrevocable: white on black. She is growing out of the dark.

The mahogany window-frames and square silvered latch
suggest that all this was some time ago: if the seats
were coloured, they would be green and blue. And nothing

has happened yet. The train could be anywhere; it makes
no difference to her. She has never heard the adage
if that's where you're going, I wouldn't start from here.

She carries herself like a chalice. Upright, a little tense,
even the hands folded in her lap are alert to catch
her basket, chance, the fluted air, and not to spill it.

Although this isn't quite the future it is still life.
She hasn't decided yet what line she will take on it,
but she looks so like herself that someone's sure to notice,

and when she arrives she will make a perfect picture in
her cobalt dress, stepping down from this east-bound train
or (if her seat faces backwards) from this train to the west.

Flight-path

Heathrow: on the map, it's enough to convince
the earth's flat as a springboard. The scarlet-edged
loops and loveknots of motorway, sliproad and fly-
over which promise all travellers (eventually)
a safe return, stumble on a runway: a loose end.

And though their steep trajectories imply
a fall, planes leave no less decisively now
than ships once went down, mercurial as fish
sky-hooked on some celestial line, each wake
a temporary gothic arc, a cartographer's pen

flourishing into the third dimension and proving
there are countries there, if only we could find them,
above the cumulus, under the light which scales
the plane's sides. Which is pure fabrication.
But new arrivals have horizons behind the eyes.

This is not, they say, *their intended destination*,
clutching about them their baggage like bedding,
their four-fold carriers, fishing-line, and the faded
black straw hat which in between-time over
the Atlantic with the sky singing like siren song

that here, but for gravity, even home might be
a place of choosing, was big enough to drown
the world in.
                    Looking down on the lights of London
settling like coins in an inverted hat's crown,
their sights are setting. They are descending (coats

trailed awkwardly as damaged wings) heavy-footed
through the great glass hall, cake-walking down
escalators and along corridors; scaling the rack
of the multi-storey in staggered and limited ascent.
They are grounded on the sliproad; they are slowly

dispersing, while overhead between planes, a long v
of Canada geese buffets in to land across the motorway,
a formation of gulls swivels like a strobe, and a glider circles,
trailing string. No one watches. They are expected;
they have arrived. At best, this is a point of departure.

Metamorphosis

I could never remember how we got there, but only
how the road was going nowhere in particular
and how the wind scudded about like litter
between car wheels when suddenly there was a barn
the size of a church and behind it the flat earth
splayed into dunes, and behind the dunes, the sea

tilted like half a balance, brimming over, self-
righting: light underwriting its surface in amber,
lime, white live wires. A closed circuit. The steps
through the dunes were concrete. The sun was very low.
We walked beside ourselves, stopgaps in the wind,
our shadows like steeple-shadows, like telegraph

poles lurching to the water's edge. Like one thing
leading to another. And the waves slopped about,
tossing out one thing or another: a plastic bottle,
a dogtoothed ball, and a piece of driftwood: a broken
wing, or arm. Under the warped growth-rings
and water-marks, a shoulderbone arrested at the turning-

point: the flesh knotting into wood, or the quick of wood
growing warm. Awkward, unfinished. You cast it off;
the sea caught and clawed it out of reach, and (silver
with salt) we gave chase. We lost it. But I remembered
how evaporated sea-water leaves traces like fish-tails.
Like lace. Like scales. Like neither one thing nor another.

Women and Secrets

(after Tirzah Ravilious)

It is the shock of absence
on waking: that shaking certainty
I heard nothing. By night, the over-
familiarity of the room oppresses: clenched
sheet, open door, and the precise proximity
of a husband's back. It was all a cover-

up: it was nothing – nothing to be spoken
of, nothing to disturb. But there are two ways
of telling. (The woman sits upright; eyes
riddle the dark.) There's a story in broken
nights, an interlude, quieter than the days'
pastiche, and more private. The simple ties

– wife, artist, mother – fall away. (Draw
the covers closer.) There's time for exploration:
motives past and present (crossed in love? a yen
for solitude?). But there's also this: not raw
psychology, but *I heard nothing.* No explanation,
but the upright jolt of waking. And then?

Love

A confidence-trick, a borrowing –
that nonchalant drop
of the shoulder under
a lover's coat. It's a way of looking:

laughing, the brightness of eye
clear as a bell –
and the swagger of the coat,
the swell of it. A certainty: each solitary

step affirms that here's a Rosalind
in Welchman's hose,
unfamiliar roughage at the neck,
and fingers rubbed on pocketed tobacco.

Here's the assurance of assumed
clothes, a landslide
in perception and identity –
a loss of self equalled only

in fever, and at time of waking:
that second's glimpse
of privacy, when the eye
opens unselved, shockingly naked.

Rumour

A boy lies at the edge of the field
with narrowed eyes and fingers
chafing the fine bladework of the grass.

And windows plane a kind of swansong
catching all the cats-paws and teeth
that splay out the grass. Then the voices:

so much for open windows. The boy
at the field's edge keeps poised
his eyes, and ears; from each voice

behind the window learns that it is
always touch and go to say
love. (The cats-paw is lost at the end

of the field. A tea-cup rattles.)
That love is a by-word, snaked
in the grass with its tune-splitting tongue.

But also this. That grass roots strongly
under the fiercest of winds,
that a banging window is nothing

to pin down – only a word that slipped:
love. Leap-footed, a sidelong
laughing in the cups. Also a song.

Perfect Pitch

Why, you've got a grip on thin air
as if it were a punt pole or a bike's
palmed accelerator, as if you could wrest
the perfect word from it, honing it down

to the marrow. You've really put your back
into this argument, and when you let rip,
yes, these are the bare bones of the case:
I'd take a punt with you out to the Marston

Ferry, dance all night and ride pillion
to Brighton with the wind cutting away
from our feet like ice. I'd cross swords.
I'd learn to fence. But above all, when you

pause and spread your hands, letting fly
a catchword with a wicked spin, I want
to give chase: I want to pick up the ball
and run with it. If this is a duel, I want to win.

It is high summer. Outside, trees are poised
on their shadows as on pedestals.
A boy circles the lawn, letting drift
a frisbee languidly from the quick-quick-

slow unhinging of his arm: a yellow disc
snickering the heat-haze. (The sky is keyed up
to a ridiculous pitch.) And fluently, as if
cutting across a line of argument or mirror

image, a second boy intercepts. Here it comes
again, almost silently. The first man feigns
a miss. One slip of the wrist and it's upon us –
preposterous, flightless, plastic fledgling

in the lecture room; cascades of glass,
torrents of abuse. And we could pick it up
and run with it (*a divine visitation, a bolt
from the blue*), and I could tell you then –

It is your turn. You hesitate. (This is a difficult
point to put across.) But now you are winging it:
the word immaculate, refined. You smile. You've
the sky in your eyes. The glass is already singing.

Landscape

Picture it like this: a length
of beach, and two people,
monochrome,
passing down the long, horizontal
reach of sea, and shadow, and sky.
How the eye
homes (almost absently) to these, figures
in landscape: the slow

movement, the caricature lilt
and drag of shadows on
sand, angled
as the hollows and rounds of speech. Love?
is its question, a hesitant
lift, quiet
as waking. The two shadows gesture, dove-
tail; words test the air

as a sleeper tries the morning
with silhouetted hand:
will it bear?
Light pours across their long silence, then
flares: the answer rises steady
as a kite,
absurd in its trust that two sticks and tissue
skin will make a bird,

flesh out the sky a little. Love:
at least half imaginative,
a question
even in reply. The two figures
edge across the beach, shadowing
new ground in
a silence which draws parallels as charged
and telling as speech.

Likeness

And if I said I saw it like this – the cut and dash
of your hands and coat-tails a marginal gloss:
the flick of the cuff and elongated index indicating
Nota, mark this well, like the showman's patter,
the smooth consecutive doodles on the surface
of the Cherwell up by the rollers before it slides
into the weir which are like so many flourishes
with silk handkerchiefs to take us all unsuspecting
up to the edge (if I said: in telling, you'd make this
sound like Niagara), these would be likenesses
as light under the bridge by the millpond takes the shape
of the wind like leaves and the volume of dark below it's
like a solid – if it weren't for that fish bowing it distractedly
and never next where it's expected, but the way pennies
dropped in a plastic washing-up bowl at a fête cut off,
glinting, at an angle, so it goes oblique, darkling from shadow
to shadow like groundswell, like the slow movement
under the surface rapids and razzmatazz of the weir. And yes,
I'd say we were both like that, and set and matched in it like
a balancing act, and always testing the water: so that if I
asked you round I'd half expect you to show with a parrot
(like out on a rope over Niagara you need a punt pole
and a scarlet silk neck-tie for distraction), and though
I've never yet found you juggling apples in Tesco I guess
if I tossed you one in passing you'd catch and flip it back
pat, like a likeness, as if you didn't even need to think.

Naming

No escaping it for Adam or Ged;
nor for Noah, ordering his neat twos
from dog-fights. I prefer Eliot's
careful withholding of the third
name for a cat. It bothers me:
what gives a namer his right?

Not love. Love is private, knows
that some kill with closeness. Naming
too's a kind of death, an over-
familiarity: *touché*. It scorches
in the giving, makes for confinement.
Thus far and no further. Look,

this is what I know. And not
knowing, or knowing too much
for abbreviation, I give you
no name but your own, intricate
and patchwork as a skin.
Yours, to carry like silence,

or a light, and all I'd dare offer,
unasked. Your unspoken name's
its inverse, a tautology private
as any cat, sudden as waking;
no claim but question, the flipped
coin balanced on its rim.

Equilibrium

I see now these last three months I've been
walking the world rimmed by your eye
like walking in Parks some day in August
when the sky skids across the grass like north
over north of two equally matched magnets,
when there's whispering in the herbaceous
border and the long line of fence is dark as
the edge of an iris. Like a child learning
suddenly to walk the barrel, like Venus
in her shell achieving an improbable balance
I have been centered: I have been whole
inches off the ground.
                          Jumping a guard-rail,
sliding down banisters, I've been treading
water in the palm of your hand, sitting pretty
as a sparrow offered up to a lightwell.
I've sensed the faint pulse of your deliberation
like the ruffling of feathers up my spine
in a soft breeze, like the stole of the sun
across my nape. How you've conjured circles
about my imagination. How our eyes skirmished
and kissed on such a high blue parabolic note
there was no holding it: we smiled off-key.
And how we shimmied to each other
like heat-haze, tearing strips off the day
and handing them over, no strings – I've pockets
full of them: thin silk rents in the fabric of things.
I suppose we knew something had to give.

So. Answer me this. Can we manage the climb-
down with equal grace? Can we bestride
the earth in a new equilibrium, and knowing it
for a disc and knowing if once we slip
whole seas will go under in the navy and gold
firmament, still swear there's a globe turning
under our feet and that it is *terra firma?*
Darling, if once you'd asked me, I'd have
jumped hard and fast as from an ice-floe.
I'd not have been responsible for the world.

Polyptych: Annunciation

I *The Art-Critic*

I wasn't noticing especially. My eyes were dazzled.
It was hot outside, and the sun was feathered
through the lights like an arrow-shaft. I must
have looked right through them. I was thinking
about the view: a clutch of bicyclists like rooks
on the tow-path, pointers of poplar out on
the horizon, a swift flicker of wings and the river
running like an uninterrupted conversation.
Closer to, an angel with a copper trumpet. I wasn't
looking at the staircase, or the people on it:
if anything, I noticed the man in a stove-pipe hat
(in the heat that day) standing by a window
in the reading room, a far-away noise like scaffolding
or a metal punt pole mishandled, and later,
when I went out, the porter sweeping up feathers,
telling me the library doesn't keep a cat.

II *The Angel*

They say this takes practice, but refuse to let us know,
till the last minute, who'll be sent for the next rehearsal:
we set off all unprepared as the Christmas Eve soloist
at King's, mouth rounded in parody of that opening *o*.
He at least has the advantage of knowing the words.
We plummet blind, like justice or liberty, coming up
below the skin of some unsuspecting mortal as if in
a diving-bell, adjusting ourselves to the cut of his spine,
the set of his eyes, and shyly glancing out at the world.
We're never told, beforehand, who it is we're looking for.
It's that, and the wings, that cause most difficulty:
we leave them off, of course, but there's no hiding
the habit of wearing them: we arch our shoulders
and stride out fast as if every other step were the point
of take-off, and our parted lips declare we are always
just about to tell... People stare. At first, though,
that day, it all seemed easy. I arrived and settled in:
not Cambridge, in fact, but the other place: the Bodleian.

A good broad stair to pace on and look out for her.
I thought the flower should be a metaphor. And then
she called me. Perhaps I was wrong – but I was sure.
And so I smiled her full in the face, and handed it over:
the seed of imagination, luminous and ready to deploy
itself between the first and second ventricle of the brain,
the stamen and filament split into the feathered warp
and weft of the double wings of a crocus vivisected
on a lightbox, roots fibrous and tentative as angel-hair.
As tow. She took it very well, I remember thinking.
She smiled straight back at me. And I fell.

III *Mary*

Of course I recognised him at once. I'd seen him before,
that boy: Renaissance man, works on the quattrocento.
Sits in the short arm of the reading room. As to why
I called him back, I'm not quite sure. He was going fast.
There was a disturbance vapoured in the air around him;
he seemed to be carrying – could they have been iris? –
and I thought he'd dropped something, so I said 'Stop –
you've forgotten your... ' '... lines?' I think he asked,
but he hadn't. Not for a minute. And I couldn't say
I wasn't expecting it. I'd been distracted all summer,
feeling my eye slip down the white channel between text
proper and marginal gloss: losing my grip. Outside
they were ringing down the scaffolding round Duke Humfrey
like a discord of outsize wind-chimes and there was a sense
of something permanently on the brink of happening
somewhere else, as when on *Morse* the choir sings *Gloria
Gloria* and corpses tumble behind the scenes. That day
in particular it was far too hot. The girl on the next desk
was strumming *Bohemian Rhapsody* under her breath;
there was a man with a pickaxe out by the sign which says
Silence Please. This is a Library; the room was humming
like a tuning-fork and the light was out of its element.
I went for a drink. He was tall in the angle of the stairs,
and I was glad, I think. All the same, afterwards at my desk,
I wondered '... so here I am, happily settled, I'd have said,
and trying to turn myself into an academic, and you come
and tell me *this*?' And what exactly? To recapitulate:
'I've forgotten my diary; I'll send you an e-mail. Perhaps

we could make a date?' And I can no more pluck the sense
from it than trace the shot of lead in the soft sift of feather-
down that's become of my heart and head, or spell my name
with this lightweight excuse of a pen I'm landed with,
which for all its strong primary bent like his silhouette
about the shoulders and its gold tip is – indubitably – a quill.

IV *Mary and the Angel*

It's no secret that God's in the details –
it's a commonplace. So when the angel
descends again, this time (a Tuesday)
in the upper reading room, it's no surprise
we concentrate on the neat brown spines
of Early English Texts or the man over by
the window in a hat like Arnolfini's
and draw the whole annunciation
irrevocably into the present tense.

So is it strange I can't always remember
your face, or only in time and place specific
locations? I've your smile at Worcester,
your chin up St Giles and cheekbones
by the faculty. But your eyes are different:
the way they throw light like darts, like a leap
of faith or the mercury twist of water tossed
from a glass, how could I possibly forget?
And I'm not sure what this amounts to, yet –

but when you swing the corner fast as a pole-
vaulter over the edge of a precipice, the ceiling
chinks like a lid under pressure and if you stop
to say *Lunch?* I'd call this room the spinning
centre of the flat earth as the roof goes up
and the scaffolding comes down in a chorus
of halleluiahs – and then you've gone.
And your face? No. Even looking I've lost it.
It's a question of focus. It's your eyes in a storm.

V *The Porter*

I can tell them at once. They're the ones whose smile
rings out like the sun cracked from a weather-vane
and whose eyes have everything to declare.
And when I search their bags – sure, they have
books, like the others, but in among the detritus
of pencils, paperclips and pens there'll be some
small thing they simply can't account for – a broken
feather, pressed crocus petal or a dusting of torn
gold-leaf. And I'll know to expect another set, come
evening, cut with the same gravity as a gown
but softer to the touch: all filaments of gossamer
silk, and swansdown. About the structure I'm less sure:
buckram, perhaps, or whalebone? I've never dissected
a pair, though we know as we take them in to lost
property it means another one's cut loose out there:
has hung up his wings for surplus, and won't be back soon.

Equivocation

After all this time I presume when we meet
face to face we will be like two apprentices
pitting themselves against the sheer weight
of a sheet of glass, the learning curve of the arms
at full stretch like an illusionist's handkerchief
before the penny drops, white-knuckled, breath
against misted breath as we try to take the measure
of this thing between us with the same shaky
precision as when you pour wine, I touch the stem
of the glass, and we glance apart: wrong-footed,
laughing, apprehensive to the fingertips. *Impasse.*

So – it's time we carried it off: tip-toe fingered,
and cheek to cheek as in a waltz while over
our heads a number ten bus goes up
like a balloon, a zebra entwines two belisha
beacons and the sky sheers off like a velux –
there's a risk, of course, but it's nothing much
to gaping across an empty space, aghast less
at the crash than the aftermath: the slack sky,
the pedestrian paces of the street stony as
denial, and flirting off round the corner of the eye,
a red rag that marks the end of a glazier's van.

Bilingual

New weight of language on the tongue;
the tongue-tied: intractable, dumb.
The mouth takes shape in a new medium.
Its own breath is less than malleable.
                        Speech becomes sculpture:
a six-month-slow baroque contortion
to form one sentence:

ik stond met m'n mond vol tanden

Sounds freshly unearthed; the mouth
furred, lichen-locked; the tongue's tip curled.
Translation's a technicality: muscular
mastery of the letter R; long division
of the plaintive seagull syllables *ee, ui, ij:*

een enkele reis, alstublieft

The first words are rotund: pristine,
hard-pressed pebbles on the tongue.
Until the moment of revelation
when they burst like grapes against
the palate, and the tongue, unleashed,
unfurls like a cat and cries: *I am loose
(los). Undone. Just look. I am translated.*

Because words are not things

In the portakabin (classroom) the master is dictating.
Words swell from deep in his stomach: purple,
tawny, and umber. They rumble about the room
like thunderclouds. The children take them down
as if they were flesh and blood words.
As if they were flesh and blood children.
There are red clouds tumbling over my head.
I look down at my neat red fountain pen.
Then: WHAM. PAF. A thick black comic strip
punchline between the eyes. A thunder-clap.
This is a word I recognise. *Komkommertje.*
I write it down. It means a small cucumber.
It doesn't sound much like a small cucumber
but like the body-language of other girls
in the playground. Clapping. Playing tag
in tidy square-toed shoes with bright
square-cut hair flapping like rags out to dry.
Kom-kom-kommertje. My hair is plaited and dull.

I look out of the window and there is a bull
in the playground. I want to say: *look, there is
a bull out in the playground*, but I don't know
the words for playground or for bull.
The bull snorts and paws the ground like a bull
in picture-books. Red smoke spurts from his nostrils
in two small thunder-clouds. He is going to charge.
I think he will charge first through the empty hall
and into the paint-store and that he'll toss his huge
head around between the shelves and PAF WHAM
his horns will prang the squishy tubes of paint
and WHAM SPLAT he will break down the door
and charge into the classroom with glutinous scarlet
and mauve and midnight blue poster paint clogging
his horns. He will stamp the floor so the classroom
(portakabin) rattles and because I don't know the words
for *scream* or *shout* or *run*, I shall have to defend
myself silently. I shall throw down my pen.

Lost and Found

On Wednesday last, in the vicinity
of the Kingston Road: item: one voice,
exact tenor and timbre unknown
but believed to be romantic (perhaps
something of a drifter). Frequently
sighted in the past by overnight travellers
on trains and coaches, in open-mouthed,
incessant, disembodied discourse
on the far side of the glass.
Believed to be making for the coast.
(Boat-owners please check your sheds.)

Its hideouts are various and it's rarely
in the same place twice but you'd know
it if you found it. It might be in the silence
when a crow stoops in a scything
graceline to pluck a leaf from the beak
of its own, moated reflection; it might be
floundering in the song sung by someone
rained on at a bus-stop, and although
you can't tell it by its gait or what it wears,
you will know it by the sense of suddenly,
incredibly, believing your own ears.

The Master-Builder

Not the birds of the air show such determination:
such a gathering of wood gathering dust gathering
good intentions. Plucked from skips, from hedges,

and the renovation of the local pub, to shape
a ramshackle wigwam in the living-room:
like jackstraws, like a life-sized game of spillikins.

Let these be the foundations, the work of the busy
right hand. Already, it has made out an architrave
and a piece of skirting. It clatters about its duty.

It is sensible. It has things to do in the kitchen.
While upstairs (six planks and a length of string)
the left hand moves mountains with a pencil.

The right hand clutches a screwdriver; the left hand
holds the house in a nutshell.
                                    Love, it says,
I have whittled you an oasis from this empty skin,

from these base red bricks and black misfirings.
The bedroom and bathroom are nave and chancel.
There will be a lightwell over the stairs where

light falls light-fingered through the chestnut tree.
The walls will be a garden, and the garden
a tapestry. We'll plant quince, crab and maple:

I've planned it to the circumference of the ripple
from the fountain.
                        In the kitchen, the right hand
extends its sore black thumb. The left hand is a poet.

The right hand has put its head in the oven.
Left hand, right hand, there is no communication.
Between them, rain moulds the bedroom ceiling

with mountain ranges splaying into tracery like leaves.
Between them, the kitchen sink has come adrift;
the house rests uneasily as a fledgling.

Both hands make shift; they take long views of things.
At night, the house lights up like a habitation.
Through the uncurtained windows there are signs

of life: a toaster, a red rose, and in every room
the intricate weft of wood that at first glance looks
something like a cross between a life-raft and an icon.

House
(after Rachel Whiteread)

Object lesson. Its walls are
Braille-blind: smooth sides of concrete in place
of windows pressed flat
as the palms of a child who wants out,
wants the collie running in the park, the long
green belt of the park itself,
the street-lights, all-night

petrol and trains that rattle-
snake the viaduct for Harwich, for
Liverpool Street. Want's
simple: *I live here. This is my home.*
A blue plaque marks the fall of the first doodle-
bug; abruptly end-terraced
number forty-six

is in scaffolding again
fifty years on, doors stuck in their jambs,
shadows sifting side-
ways with a sandtimer tilt behind
blinds. Up the road number 193 is railed:
opaque as a monument,
looking-glass chimney

breasts too straight-forward for words.
(*What for? – Why not?*) Even the trace-marks
of the stairs are one-
dimensional as an unravelled
palimpsest. It's as if memory could be
cast whole, and a house reduced
to its logical

elements, as if it weren't
more: the fierce and fragile habit of
belonging, footsteps
persisting in their pattern even
under scaffolding, slipping as fluently
as any cat or burglar
through blocked doors, over

the invisible paper
roses on the walls, and up and out
through the skylight. Filled
and sealed: an absence so tangible
it is itself a kind of hoarding; the park
no park but *the view*
from here, even as

ball and chain weigh slowly in,
the suddenly empty air runs rings
round the child calling
his dog and the grass stretches without
interruption to the railway and
the dark, marginal doodle
that is the canal.

Travelling Light

Like flotsam curtseying on the spot, things
are coming back to him. Honeysuckle. Lavender.
The weighty press and scent of blackcurrant
bushes as he walked out, and his mind edgy

as a cat testing the sun, all vertebrae.
A five-runged swimming-pool ladder hung
from a brick garden wall, but no pool.
How this (more than anything) irked him.

And the way the village High Street dead-ended
in *Danger Cliff Fall Road and Path Destroyed*
and someone had raised the red and white
barrier to an arch, and someone was growing roses.

How the last house that day was aerial –
yellow tin butterfly roof open to the sky,
marram grass coiled in chicken wire and a wall
of railway sleepers topped with blue and green

bottles like skittles, like a seismograph – and how
the breakwater below crissed and double-crossed
before coming up with a red flag with an air of
surprised finality. Why he took it for an omen,

so when the plane strummed over and its propeller
cut a corkscrew spiral like the final flourish in
a game of consequences or conclusive proof
that air is thicker than water he looked askance

at the barricade and for *Danger* read *Dance*
and brushed past the roses to step out in
its wake lightly as a cat with artful insouciance
ringing down the ladder onto the lawn.

Skelton and the Birds

'Words are swords, and hard to call again.'

Easier than he'd thought possible,
the old ventriloquist's trick of slipping
his skin. Even as his mind *in extremis*
turned in on itself like a flock of doves,
it was still at his finger-tips; his hands
in the folds of his cassock feathering

the hawk, the parrot and the sparrow.
He went down to the river.
He'd imagined being stranded there
for hours, like the man with a boat
and three incompatibles (fox, goose
and cabbage), but despite its talk

of liberty, only the parrot was slow
on the uptake. He tossed it a date.
And it was then the ferryman saw him
(an old man skimming pebbles) and took
his raised hand for a summons.
Startled, inarticulate, the parrot took wing:

rumour made flesh. (*Thy words are wind,
never have they no weight.*) But for all
his promised silence, there was talk
later of a falcon over London Bridge
and a streak of green among the ravens
at the Tower. Even that day, the ferryman

said the air about him was turbulent;
the watch on the gate gave a double challenge
(*who goes there, who?*) and as he paused
before turning away he thought he heard
a voice somewhere down on the river
chaffing *Feather, you little goose, feather.*

Skelton at Diss

As for what they dredged from the mere
two days ago: of that, as of many things,
he will remain silent. Neither fish,
fowl, nor good red herring, but fleshly
proof the old Scots allegation is true:
Englishmen have tails. As for Christian
burial, he will leave that to the sexton.

It has grown difficult even to pray.
In nomine patri – but the wind is incarnate:
it is inside his head and torments there
like a caged bird. He can sense
the shape of it: walks his own mind
gingerly, not to startle it, as daily
he must edge around the mere.

He knows now: there was no miracle.
When Christ walked on water it was
purely practical. There's no going straight
anywhere round here, but always instead
a soughing over-shoes in mud with only
the wind for support. It rings hollow.
A slipper hold the tail is of an eel.

It's not the edginess that bothers him.
He has been to Yarmouth and seen
the sky tethered off behind the horizon
like a loose canvas flap. He has seen
the herring-catch brought in and thought
that words used to be like that:
illumined silver, quick-still, runnel-backed

and in profusion, which now are sparse,
wind-whittled: brittle dead wood. He talked
to fishermen about tides and erosion,
and saw that to write again, would mean
to write in short sentences. The tongue
a pillar of salt, the self a walking contradiction:
breathless, and laureate. He returned to Diss.

The wind cut and thrust like a courtier;
the sky settled like a weight on his back.
And it was then he found them,
his congregation, hummocked round
the mere like fallen angels, and they glummed
on him and parted ranks to show him
their catch. He heard himself pray

with words that came straight from the tongue
though his mind disremembered them
and in insistent non-sequitur pictured how
only the day before, some hunting parson's
hawk had stooped and left by the west door
a clutch of grey tail feathers and the single
immaculately shorn-off wing of a pigeon.

First Light

They set out early and the light was poor.
After the first full roar, the diesel settled down
to a steady off-beat (like a heart) somewhere near
their feet. They couldn't see it for the mist; even
the rudder in their hands cut off like a question-mark.
That first night they moored the canal was full of noises.
Crocodile, they said. *War-ship, flying fish* – because this
was their honeymoon, and nothing could be only itself
that was also part of their story. And later when there was
an odd whistling like a kettle with its throat cut
and a thumping on the roof as if someone was trying
to board, they said *Pirates. Or fish. With knives in their teeth.*
Marauders – but in the morning found they'd tied up
by an orchard and under the mist the canal was a wash
of apples (red as apples at a fairground) which parted for
a swathe of cygnets that swam whistling *between the teeth*:
a high dry sound, thin as paper. They took it for an omen
(as if it were a wind; as if the boat had sails, or wings)
although the sun seen through clouds was shifty as moonshine,
and they were puzzled several times by an angular creaking
sound that might have been a heron.
                      Then they settled down: they worked out
a routine for locks and tip-up bridges; they adopted a cat
and called it Owl. They grew used to the boat's only half-
perceptible buoyancy (they said their feet had fins), to non-
resistance when they passed through a town. To quarries,
tree-houses, ironworks and the different sorts of boundary
between gardens. To the noise of trains after dark,
to a sense of weight loss and the grey area between canal
and solid ground – but without markers it was hard to tell
when buoyancy became a habit, when there were still
sunsets of a sort but nothing much to say about them,
or who it was first thought they'd overshot the heron
and who replied that although they could tie up anywhere
they liked, the canal has nothing that might be called
a port and precious little room to turn around.

Hawk Point

No hawks ever, though overcome on first arrival
by the static between beach and sun (each grain
of sand a ravelled-up rainbow) it's easy to mistake
for one the underlit, spreadeagled v of a gull's back
with its wingtips flexed to an index. But no one

could read the slipshod cast-off a gull has in tow
for the bullet of concentration that's the shadow
of a hawk: the dark alive and steady as a pupil.
Lizards, though, there may be, in quick-fire lassitude
on an outcrop, and always, the catch-and-drag of

the cliff-path gate, pyramidal shards of beech underfoot
and cabbala of light like water coursing through the leaves:
patches of blue string the nut-walk like handkerchiefs,
and at the end of the wood, the cliff drops away
and the sky's a buoyancy (no hawks ever,

but a glider, cherry-red, bellies fish-like over). The air's
sluggish as water on the sea-bed; the heat's intense.
Lying in longitude on a rock and flickering under the fork-
tongued eddy of wind, the eye's a pupil to the horizon's
iris; two stems of couch-grass angle like a sextant

and encompass the sky's whole circumference until
the index nail pierces and peels them against the ball
of the hand so the sprung green furls about
the sand's opalescence and the ultra of the marine
like the blades of glass at the eye of a marble –

and this is what it boils down to: a seascape
in the round between forefinger and thumb.
Inland, when the falconer raises a focus for his eagle-
owl, her head runs rings about it: the ellipses narrow
until she has it stilled, like a pupil to her pupil.

From Barbara Hepworth's Garden

This photograph was taken through the eye
of the sculpture, where water lies cupped
like a fleck of light on the retina, reflecting
the bronze which reflects elements of the sky.

The eye fragments. Beyond it are pieces of visitors
to the garden: half a body, an uncapped head,
an arm. They are hard to follow. The eye
gives a restricted view. (From the street below

the garden itself is invisible.) Lying back
in a black and white shell of a chair in
the conservatory – just out of the picture –
a voice circles phrases, lazily, like smoke rings,

like paper birds. The visitors are passing (one
with an orange rucksack). They are standing up,
they are moving away from the edge of this snap-
shot they have no part in. The voices continue.

There is no interruption.

The town is staggering up the hill. The people
are climbing up the town. They are flying kites
from the burial mounds on Trencrom.
Children run rings round the Men-an-Tol.

On the south coast above Newlyn bay, all
the maidens have turned to stone, *the earth
rising and becoming human.* The sea grinds
sand for its shores; the land is its own elegy.

(*There is no interruption.*)

Moving upwards and inland, away from the kites
and the sea, the voices grow dissonant.
The garden is fading in the sun. Its shadows
are monolithic: like stone, colouring differently

under different carvers' hands. And this is the art
not the photograph of memory: the need to rebuild,
repeatedly, the smile on the living face, to cradle it
like china, looking *not back in time, but through it*

like water: in the hand, a snapshot, in the workshop
a sculpture wanting form. There is life in it. It will
cut to the quick. The form is pierced. The eye is full
of water. Reflections rain from the sky like hammer-blows:

solidly, and without interruption.

Life-writing

It is a matter of questioning. The bare essentials:
Hieroglyph. Photograph. Reportage. Memory.
At twelve she climbed trees.
        Her hands were ringed
In earth, clay; diamond, emerald, or opal.
She had a husband and two sons.
She had two gardens, she loved travel.
Auburn-haired, she'd have liked to wear orange.
She'd tumble downhill to save her hat from a pond.
A clutch of facts: *obiter*, incidental.
Beneath, there's a shelf-life shaping:
A shadow-self. Space at the centre of a ring.
Under cupboards, lost thread spins its colours
In darkness; in darkness glasses lustre to themselves.
        And the moral is –
Unfathomable. This is not a story;
It's a balance of probabilities and plans.
        Turn her mugs in the sun:
Revolutionary, ringed, it's as close as she'll come.
        This is a kind of equilibrium:
Absence contained. The laying on of hands.
The light grows fractious as mosaic.
There is work in progress. It is provisional.

Shelf-life

These are the parings of a life, the incidentals
Which flake away as a potter parts dry
Waste clay from her pot.
        Leaving bare essentials:
Kiss and kick of shoe on a spinning disc,
Sunlight cobwebbed, sagging across the shed.
The potter says it's a question of centring.
Her leg swings from the knee, her wheel spins
Like the flat earth on its invisible axis:
She throws clay plumb as the first stone
Or a brilliant guess. Lifeless, it spins.
        She cups her hands, pools
The cool, revolutionary weight of it.
It evolves expansively. Elastically. Spinning.
Bulk in indigo shade; highlight tipped.
        The room is very quiet.
Her hands take the pot's runnelled imprint
        Containing, self-contained
She stoops, considers.
        Yes, provisionally
The pot is done.
        The wheel slows.
The room settles like dust in the sun.

(for Jessica Lilian Griffiths, née Broad, 1909-1987)

Speech
(for R.E.G., 1910-1991)

Long periods, these. The voice rises,
falls down a century, careful
in its questions of time, and spacing.
His hands set the pace, tracing
lines of thought, cradling his subject
like string. Lights

and shadows, these movements of a voice,
balancing the black, the off-white.
He lets them sink to conclusion. Hands
lie pooled in the shade of his lap;
the diver in its glass bottle dips:
a bright slip-

stream in the water's darkness. He angles
with the straight pins of speech, bent on
a needle-point of light in the mind's
opaque eye. His hands lift, the palms
open. The diver plumbs glassy depths.
Bubbles rise

like questions, open endings of thought,
but a sentence falls, bottoms out.
Watch through the glass: it is a sharp-edged
penny that cuts through water lightly as
through the conjuring hand, coin on coin
till towers

rise between his fingers. He plies them
round a small space of air, his voice
shaping true, and false, as he pays out
his conjectures. There is a pause.
Then the answer forms. The diver bobs,
and rises.

The Art of Memory

First, you must choose a system, any system.
Think of a wall. Divide it
(like the backdrop of an early theatre)
into five parts: the first tall and thin,
the others, square. Now, fix each with
an image, any image.
Traditionally a ship
and obelisk would appear, but if you'd prefer
choose a spinning-top, take a goldfish.

Next, select those things you want to remember:
a small glass fox, Blackfriars Bridge
(early morning, with sunlight scything off
the dome of St Paul's), a pub garden
embrace. Lift them, carefully, one
by one, and pin each of them
to a memory-place, as
a child blindfold at a party pins the donkey's
tail. Stand back; watch patterns develop.

The method's never been known to fail. Look. Here
is the bridge. Rehearse it; walk
round it; walk underneath, along the sleek
purling muscle of the river,
along the belly-side of things. Snake-
skin dapplings reflect and warp
the riveted steel girders
which support dry land's smooth progression over
mooring posts, over acanthus leaves

flourishing on the capitals of phalanxed
Corinthian columns gone
astray (the piers for an absent railway,
mammoths shouldering thin air). Note that
the view from the bridge overleaps them.
Then move on. Here's the house where
Wren watched St Paul's grow buoyant
in the first floor drawing-room window, and below
in the garden is a pool heavy

with goldfish, and apple trees in silhouette
overlaid on the clean cut,
obeliskesque powerstation's profile,
over the precise, diamond-hinged
geometries of cranes lifting thatch
for the great Globe's rebuilding
(Bankside and Rose Alley grown
ankle-deep in reed), lifting time hesitantly,
swinging, reversing the pendulum

weighted by a clutch of straws, and containing,
roofing in the tiring-house
wall. Architecting time. (Downstream under
the river on a long red carpet
Brunel raises a glass: *to progress*,
and twelve dozen reflected
candle-flames wrap themselves round
the bowl.) And all the while the people are passing:
awkward, unfathomable, moving

people, with briefcases, bags, or three balls of
string. Behind them is St Paul's.
They flicker past the balustrade like gold-
fish in the sun; they pause in the bays
to exchange views. Doors open and shut.
The river cuts and shuffles
light, the spoken words eddy:
freighted, evanescent, impassable. Cross-
currents, consequences, will run and run.

Abstract

I

He must have painted it that first
day abroad: white square
on a white background, the sun
rising solidly
against his bedroom wall. White noise:
an early train syphoning

over the viaduct, and five
clean syllables as
a man calls his dog. The sun
on the balcony
is almost audible; below,
the city is abroad, is

uncontainable. The window
flows over with it.
Say it's six a.m., and light.
The paving stones are too small;
the narrow houses
are straight up and down, all surface
without shadow. The windows

are curtained white. Say it's abroad.
It must reduce to
a question of texture, eye-
catching and abstract,
white square against a white background
on a white gallery wall.

II

The gallery itself would make
a composition:
on the right, an imbalance
of white squares and just
off-centre a dark dividing
line, its exterior glass

wall that's a formal point of rest.
Outside, the may swings
like a reflection; blackbirds
chatter in some high-
pitched tongue. The stream flings up broken
squares of light. On its bare

mesh, the painting's square-tipped brushstrokes
compose, optically,
a kind of disillusion.
The square in its two
dimensions is more solid than
the canvas which supports it,

more solid than the outside wall.
It's a breathing-space,
the artist at rest.
It's the cage which sings
and not the bird; it's sunlight on
his walls that first day abroad.

Parallel Motion

In the front room of the fourth-floor apartment
overlooking the harbour, a clock slowly pays out
one thin gold chain; slowly retracts the other

like a spider drawing float-lines back into its belly.
It is all face and no body: it hardly looks serious enough
to keep time. All doors in the flat have frosted glass

panels; the clock goes naked. At night its round white
moonface catches the lights from across the harbour;
looking back from Lion Bridge, each uncurtained window

holds an identical white dimple above the almost perpetual,
almost silent movement of the chains. On each floor
a clock modestly goes through the motions of gravity.

Behind the scenes, lifts rise with becoming gravity
on pulleys housed between the walls of the fourth floor.
Each night the apartment thrums with perpetual

motion. Wheels turn within walls, and each window
reflects the contained electric storm that is the harbour:
water rolling darkly as thunder with shimmering white

inverted highlights of neon; rain falling like glass,
the windows dazzled with rain. There is water enough:
the river pulses through town like a snake on its belly

between embankments, bearing tugs, barges, and all its other
traffic high above the houses. The lift hits sea-level about
the first floor. The clock hangs like a bubble in the apartment.

A poem against the kind of occasional verse

which starts with a long quavering line like the run-up
to a marginal doodle on a set of lecture notes, the sort
which starts as a circle, becomes an eye, grows a quiff
and some flowers which sprout from an enormous ear
that's attached to a retrospective tea-pot spout
and culminates in a set of legs like those which belong
to an occasional table of the unassuming kind which
can always be pushed (almost) to one side: not just because
it's a way of running a paperchase single-handed so even
the element of surprise is lost or because the ends of lines loiter
without intent like drunks on the pavement at closing-time but
mainly because of the pretence that the writer is simply
part of the scenery, part of a bar-stool or a swift triangle
of red skirt round the ellipse of the Sheldonian who has stumbled
upon herself as upon the occasional table or chair leg
and observed herself and written her down, unassuming
and pi as the artless voice on the telephone whispering
it's only me when really *it is I* all the time.

Errata

Page 1, line 8, for incorrigible read unredeemable
Page 5, line 9, for undeniable read indelible
Page 6, line 15, for unreliable read untellable

Dark, and the lights are out in all the houses.
The one streetlamp is swamped in sycamore,
all the hill's houses are cradled in root.
Leaves' shadow-selves crowd the walls like ivy.
The dark is laying it on thick, tonight.

Page 16, line 5, for untellable read unspeakable

The cat by the cellar window is a cat-shaped
absence, in black. The cellar window's a strip-light
at its feet, a chink: the earth opening up.
The air is sticky as ink.

Page 20, line 10, for supplicate read deny
Page 20, line 12, for deny read supplicate

Suppose the man in the cellar looked up,
he'd only see dark behind the darker spikes
of lavender and rosemary. (The cat is quite invisible.)
And he doesn't look up. He is exchanging words
painstakingly. Dust and ink lodge indelibly
in his thumb; it ghosts to its negative, a thumbprint.
He will leave his mark. He works in the half-dark
almost all night. Letter by letter, he is setting things right.

Page 22, line 3, for unspeakable read unjustifiable

He is locking up, he is getting a grip on this story
(the press with its oil-black rollers is waiting),
taking the lead weight of it between two hands,
tilting its lead-black against the ink-black
of the window; taking the first, fresh, impression.

Page 38, line 4, for simulate read assimilate
Page 40, line 2, for clarify read uncurtain

The first principle of design is leaving things out,
is in the spacing and the margins. Seven years
is the time-span for a complete change of skin.

Page 53, line 9, for past read future
Page 54, line 5, for amend read alter
Page 58, line 2, for alter read correct
Page 61, line 6, for correct read impose

The lines are unjustified. The errors are spawning.

Page 61, line 8, for impose read query
Page 62, line 5, the bracket should be closed
after the evidence, not after as clearly.

The chase frames the story.
Time and place are composed.

In the room above, a cat tests the floorboards.
It is six o'clock. It is almost morning.
Street-lights turn yellow; the sky comes adrift.
Clouds scud loose and dirt as newsprint.
The house will wake soon. Soon things will happen:
words will be exchanged: irrevocable, unredeemable,
demanding another night's work, and another, over-writing.

Page 70, line 2 for unjustifiable read unrevisable

There are not enough spaces between the days.

The Biographies of Poets

As always, it's a question of beginnings.
Born. In Letchworth, in Darlington. In nineteen
forty-two, or nineteen sixty-nine. Educated.
Attempts to educate were made. Initially
wrote, took up the pen, was published
in a large number of small magazines:
as always, acknowledgements are due

to the following and to the photographer
for the cropped chiaroscuro mug-shot
which you, the reader, scan for clues
or revelations beyond the black and white
lines, the changing dedications. Currently
(always) lives with husband, cat or lover.
Gardens, drinks, teaches: divides time.

Since the birth of their first child, runs
cooks swims; has taken to seeing things
between the cracks in the ceiling.
Whether in London Wales or Devon, wakes
daily, wearing the body as crumpled
linen, brimming with words like spirit,
like wine. Preserves, pickles, divides time

like water, senses its parting, currently,
into live wires, barley-twist columns, scales
of light: conceives vocab in response.
Since divorce paints skates jogs, collects
egg-cups, writes biographies (inverted
prisms). Luciferous, and flowing over with life
like water, like salt, sand, or wine.